Stick Your Neck Out

An Invitation and Guide to House Church Planting

Travis Kolder

Copyright © 2021 Travis Kolder

All rights reserved. This book or any portion thereof may not be reproduced or used in any manner whatsoever without the express written permission of the publisher except for the use of brief quotations in a book review or as permitted by law. Please contact the author at www.traviskolder.com for reproduction requests.

Unless otherwise indicated, all Scripture quotations are taken from the Holy Bible, New Living Translation, copyright © 1996, 2004, 2015 by Tyndale House Foundation. Used by permission of Tyndale House Publishers, a Division of Tyndale House Ministries, Carol Stream, Illinois 60188. All rights reserved.

Scripture quotations marked (ESV) are from The ESV® Bible (The Holy Bible, English Standard Version®), copyright © 2001 by Crossway, a publishing ministry of Good News Publishers. Used by permission. All rights reserved.

First printing, 2021

You can reach the author at:

www.traviskolder.com

@traviskolder (Twitter)

Facebook.com/traviskolder

Table of Contents

Introduction	1
Chapter 1: Stick Your Neck Out	3
Chapter 2: The Glory of Christ and the Planting of Many House Churches	11
Chapter 3: The Calling of Christ	17
Chapter 4: An Easily Planted Church	25
Chapter 5: Character That Carries a Movement	37
Chapter 6: Calling Forth the Women	49
Chapter 7: Wanted: Workers for the Harvest	59
Appendix A: When Not to Start a House Church	63
Appendix B: Further Reading	65
Notes	67
About the Author	71

Introduction

Seismic shifts are taking place in the global church. Much of the church is falling more in love with Jesus, becoming simpler, and focusing more on making disciples. But if you would have told me in 2019 that one of the places in the Earth where that shift would happen was right here in the United States, I don't know if I would have believed you.

COVID-19 has changed all that.

Regularly, I meet with friends who were active participants of traditional churches in the beginning of 2020 but who are now struggling with church. They realize that church is more than what they can get on a webstream or even at a meeting where people gather, sing worship songs, and listen to preaching. They long for a spiritual family.

Recently, I met a new friend who came to a gathering where I spoke about our experience related to house churches. She came up to me afterward in tears. Her traditional church had closed during the pandemic and never reopened. She was hungry to experience God with a group of people again but didn't know where to find that. We prayed for her and connected her with a group of believers who were meeting together.

And she's not alone. Many of us across the western hemisphere and around the world are experiencing a similar phenomenon. In the United States, 2020 has taught us two incredibly important truths: First, small, reproducible items (and actions) have huge consequences. If you were unclear about what "going viral" meant before 2020, you can now see that reality play out in front of you on a daily basis. We've known that viruses spread, but we have rarely felt the impact of that the way we have this year. I believe that what we've seen with COVID-19, as terrible as it's been, is a picture of how the gospel of Jesus and small, reproducible churches can spread quickly to those who need it most. The urgent question around this lesson is this: If a small virus can turn the world on its head, what could the gospel of Jesus do if it were allowed to go viral in the Earth?

Second, we've learned the difficult lesson that church—not crowds assembled to hear preaching and singing but the actual community of God gathering around his presence and sharing life together—is critical to the Christian walk. We don't just need sermons and songs; we need the community that happens when believers encourage one another, pray for one another, and hold each other accountable. We are learning that church as we know it is much different than church as God wants it. The urgent question here is this: If church the way God designed it is essential to the life of believers, how do we become that church?

The pages that follow are an attempt to answer both of these questions. If you, like many people I know, are rethinking church in this season, I'd invite you to read along. God has an answer for your ache within. It's not an easy answer. It's not even a safe answer. But the journey that these answers will take you on is worth the cost.

So join me. You won't regret it.

Chapter 1: Stick Your Neck Out

Then, calling the crowd to join his disciples, he said, "If any of you wants to be my follower, you must give up your own way, take up your cross, and follow me."
~ Mark 8:34

The death and resurrection of Jesus launched the beginning of the most powerful movement the world has ever seen, a movement unlike any other in history. The world has never been the same. In one bold move, Jesus released the life of God onto the planet.

His next act was to do something scary, something so radical, that if we hadn't heard the stories, we never would have believed it. God entrusted the DNA of the life of heaven to ordinary humans. Don't just gloss over that. Don't read it and move on. Jesus was resurrected, sure. But he had to go away. It was better that he left. (See John 16:7.)

In a bold move, he left this new movement that had culminated in his resurrection in the hands of a bunch of guys who didn't have it together. They were the plumbers of their day, the garbage collectors, the nurses, and the used car salesmen. They were the Al Qaeda terrorists and the IRS agents (literally). Sometimes, they were concerned about prayer and casting out demons, and the next minute, they were concerned about which of them would be the greatest.

Did I mention they were mostly teenagers? Did I mention that almost all of them had quite recently promised loyalty to

Jesus forever, only to take off as soon as some Roman guards showed up? Did I mention the one that seemed like the most obvious choice for leader had just denied Jesus three times in one night? Most people in their right minds would question Jesus's choice of these people.

But these same men had been with him for three-and-a-half years. They had seen the miracles. They had lived life with him. They had heard him teach. In fact, they had done more than listen to his teaching; they had been infected with the lifestyle of heaven.

And like all infections, this good news about Jesus as king swept through Asia, Europe, and Africa. It did not require educated people, dedicated buildings, or even complete Bibles. The message of "Jesus is Lord" would move from person to person with the aid of the Holy Spirit through people who had no idea what they were doing. The message was "caught" and then "passed."

All this was done through ordinary people who left their ordinary lives to become part of something greater. Jesus began a movement that we call the church through men with names like Peter, Thomas, and James. He continued that process through people named Paul, Steve, and Phoebe. Today, he uses guys named Justin, Chris, and Jose and girls named Ariel, Chantel, and Ling. My point is that he wants to use you.

Yes, you.

This good news was meant to "go viral," and the main way Jesus designed this message to spread was between ordinary people. You may not have been told this, but the moment you accepted Jesus as Lord of your life, you became part of the process for that message to pass on to someone else. You became infected with a Jesus virus and will spread it wherever you go.

You are an important part of God's plan. You with all your imperfections. You with all your hang-ups. The unorganized you. The you who doesn't quite have it together. You.

That is a scary thought. But scarier still is the fact that I am asking you to do something besides just signing up for an email list. I want you to do more than sign up for children's ministry at your church or even just donate money.

I'm asking you to leave the comfort of everything you've ever done in the past and become a part of this Jesus virus spreading all over the planet. I am asking you—yes, you!—to infect other people with the message of Jesus, teach them how to respond to it, and help them become carriers of this same Jesus virus.

This process of infecting, cultivating, and spreading has a name in Christianity. It's called church planting. And it's time for you to get involved.

Planting Churches—Me?

Right now, everything inside you will tell you that you could never start a church. No way. But check that thought at the door and stay with me for just a few minutes.

What I am not asking you to do is go to seminary, get a band together, or start writing sermons. If that is the sort of church you have in mind when you hear the words "start a church," then I would expect you to quit.[1] No, I am asking you to start a church that is so simple, nearly anyone can do it with some help.

The church I am describing is totally consumed with Jesus. They eat, sleep, and dream about him. He is more important than the building you meet in or what you say when you get together. The church that you are helping to start is held together by him alone. He brings the church together, you talk about him when you come together, and he is the life force empowering you when you meet and when you go out from your times together.

If it sounds as if I am talking about the church as if it's a group of people instead of a place or a meeting, it's because I am. You see, the church that you are planting is a group of people who are consumed with Jesus. They are not bound together by a building, an event, or a brand but as a people who live life together, seeking Jesus and following him. They are beginning to walk out a 24-7 relationship with Jesus together as a spiritual family. For this church, no place or time is sacred except every place and time when they get together.

Why are these people so consumed with Jesus? Hopefully, they are all believers who deeply understand what Jesus has done for them. But I also hope that they are people who have come to believe in Jesus because you told them about him. Part of the reason for starting a church is to lead people to Jesus. As the lost people you know hear about Christ and desire to follow him, they naturally become a part of your spiritual family. You teach them to live out this relationship with Jesus day in and day out. As you do, more people come to Christ. And what started with you and maybe one or two other believers has become a group of ten to fifteen people so awestruck by what God has done that they regularly gather to talk about Jesus and encourage each other to continue to follow him.

Buildings, sermons, and events just to check off the appropriate boxes have little meaning because Jesus draws these people together. Church has become so simple that anyone who knows Jesus can participate. Everything that would keep an untrained or unskilled man or woman, like the apostles Peter and John (Acts 4:13), from starting churches has been removed. Church has become so simple that anyone, including you, can organize it.

Now imagine if churches like these, ten to fifteen in number, meeting simply, walking out the life of Jesus together, were to begin to grow. First, Jesus begins to move on two or three people in the church about the lost people in a neighborhood or workplace. Those few are sent to start another church like yours to reach the lost. With your support, that church begins to grow. Then it happens again. And again. Soon, we are talking about multiple churches that are starting new churches that will start still more new churches.

You might not be part of this type of church right now, but you might plant one. And the church you start could be a seed for a movement of churches, bringing people to Christ all around the globe. Yes, you could start an entire movement.

Because that is what happens when the church begins to work the way it's supposed to. Those that start as part of your church are the seeds for the next two or three churches. And then those churches will carry the seeds for two or three more churches. Like all living things, your church and the churches that come from them will give birth to other churches.

This all happens because the truth of the gospel has taken root in your soul, and you have become contagious. You pass on the things of the kingdom to others. You are equipping them to pass on what they are receiving from you.

Why is this important? Billy Graham, the famous American evangelist who has led millions of people to Jesus, was once asked what his strategy would be if he were a local minister. His response was that he would pour his life into a group of men for a few years and have those men do the same thing.[2] His inspiration for the idea was the discipleship process that Jesus used.

The apostle Paul learned the same thing from Jesus. He told Timothy that his job was to take the things he had heard Paul teach and teach them to faithful men who would teach others the same thing. (See 2 Timothy 2:2.) The torch continually passed from one believer to another. The goal was not just that the truth would be passed to the next person but that the truth would be passed to a person Paul had never met, and that person would pass it on.

And this is part of the reason the church in China has gone from 700,000 believers in 1950 to 21 million or more in this century.[3] They believe that every believer is called to share the gospel, make disciples, and plant churches. As Alan Hirsch paraphrases, one of their sayings is "Every believer a church planter, every church a church planting center."[4]

This will not be easy. You will have to be willing to go places no one has gone. You will have to live among people that will make the religious crowd question your judgment. You will be teaching people whose lives are falling apart how to access Jesus and put their lives back together again. This is not a call to a comfortable upper- or middle-class Christianity. All of this will require you to be brave.

You see, starting churches that reproduce anywhere among unfamiliar people is not easy or safe. It's truly a dangerous act. You are challenging Satan on his turf and stealing people from his kingdom. Demons will need to be cast out. Sicknesses will need to be healed. Others may persecute you.

These people that come to Christ will have their own struggles. You will walk them through their sin and help them to trust Christ as both their Savior and sanctifier. Some will fall away, which will break your heart. Some will succeed beyond your wildest dreams, which brings with it a new set of challenges. Some will face unprecedented hardships planting churches. From the highest of highs to the lowest of lows, you will have to lay down your life and your comfort for all their sakes.

For you, this means embracing the lifestyle of Jesus and the apostles. Jesus left his Father in heaven and became a man. He became subject to the weakness of men and the temptation of sin to point people to a God who loved them. Likewise, the apostles left their parents, their fishing boats, and their tax booths and set out on the journey of a lifetime. They left everything for the sake of the message that had changed them. Your journey will ask you to do the same.

This road ahead will be difficult. There will be days and nights of prayer and fasting. There will be relational struggles and endless meetings. There will be threats from the mission field you serve. Scariest of all, if you have a spouse or children, they will be in this fight with you, and the bullets aimed at you might hit them.

But what motivated the apostles and what will sustain you is Jesus. He is the great treasure that we gain, and that treasure is worth more than anything we lose. Because he gave up his life, we willingly embrace the cross of this lifestyle that comes with starting churches.

So I urge you, brothers and sisters, to join me on this journey. Become so consumed with Jesus and his love that you can't help but share the gospel with lost and broken people. Help those who come to Christ become the church as God designed it to be. And teach them to start the same kinds of churches you've started. It will not be easy, but Jesus makes it worthwhile.

I am asking you to take a risk and do something adventurous with your life. Leave boredom and mediocrity behind. Step out and do something that will only make sense in light of the resurrection of Jesus. Join me on the dangerous path of planting house churches among the lost and the broken.

I'm asking you, dear brothers and sisters, to stick your neck out.

Chapter 2: The Glory of Christ and the Planting of Many House Churches

You are not your own, for you were bought with a price. So glorify God in your body.
~ 1 Corinthians 6:19–20 ESV

His body [is] the fullness of him who fills all in all.
~ Ephesians 1:23, author's paraphrase

Jesus walked into your life and changed you. He transferred you out of the kingdom of darkness into the kingdom of God. This did not just happen because you came to your senses one day.

Jesus, from the beginning of time, had planned to come to Earth, live a sinless life, and die on a cross, all to redeem you from sin and death. Then, by the Holy Spirit, he sought you out and won your heart.

The result is a new life in him that he purchased for you. He freed you from fear, torment, guilt, death, and destruction now and in the life to come. Whether or not your conversion was dramatic, your old life of death ended and a new life, unlike anything you could imagine, began.

But he didn't do this just so that you could live however you wanted. You were a slave redeemed from one master (Satan) and purchased by a new master. Paul says this: "Give yourselves completely to God, for you were dead, but now you have new life. So use your whole body as an instrument to do what is right for the glory of God.... Previously, you let yourselves be slaves to impurity and lawlessness, which led ever deeper into sin. Now you must give yourselves to be slaves to righteous living so that you will become holy" (Romans 6:13, 19).

This new life that you have received has a point to it. You went from being a slave of sin to being a slave of God. He purchased your life with his own. This purchase was so rare, so devastatingly costly to the God of the universe, so all-encompassing and generous of him, that the only logical conclusion is for you to use what's left of your time on the planet to glorify him. Paul again has said it so well: "You were bought with a [great] price. So glorify God with your body" (1 Corinthians 6:19–20 ESV).

Friends, the only reasonable response to the gospel of Jesus Christ is to glorify God. But if that's true, how do we do it?

What Does It Mean to Glorify God?

The subject of God's glory and glorifying him permeates the pages of the Bible. First, God is glorious. As the originator and creator of all things, he is separate from and above every other created thing. Glory is an intrinsic part of who he is.

Second, God shows us his glory. Throughout history, God has shown up and displayed his glory to mankind. Many times, miraculous events occur that demonstrate God's goodness and his absolute out-of-this-world nature. In the Old Testament, God's glory frequently showed up in a cloud, in a pillar of fire, or through other supernatural manifestations.

The writers of the New Testament tell us that while God continued to show up in miraculous, mind-bending ways, the most complete way God has shown us his glory was in his Son. One writer says Jesus "radiates God's own glory and expresses the very character of God" (Hebrews 1:3). So while we still will have supernatural encounters in this life, Jesus is the final, most exact expression of the glory of God.

Third, when we encounter God's glory, he changes us. (See

2 Corinthians 3:18.) We who have received him have entered a new reality. John tells us this new reality transforms us. Because we see him, we become like him (1 John 3:2). We are being transformed into the image of Jesus. This is not a one-time event but one continuous transformation, changing us from the inside out.

This brings us to the last type of glory: glorifying him. Since Christ has not just saved you but dwells in you by his Spirit, others will notice. Your life is submitted to Jesus as king, and announcing his kingship will turn the heads of others. Others will notice this internal transformation. Hopefully, they will give their lives to him as a result. The glory of God that started as part of him and moved into you is now moving into others. We glorify God by seeing his glory, receiving his glory, and reflecting it to others.

Missionary Glory

Finally, Paul understood that glorifying God could happen anywhere, and he had a particular burden to reach those who had never had an opportunity to see it. The message of the good news and this glory had to be shared in places they had never been. (See Romans 15:7–22.)

Paul was not content to keep this glory to himself. None of us should be. Jesus himself said that we were a city set on a hill so that the entire world would glorify God by our good deeds (Matthew 5:14). There are a lot of ways to glorify God, but one aspect of how God gets glory is through the spreading of the gospel everywhere in every way.

God is committed to spreading his glory across the Earth. He said to the prophet Habakkuk, "For as the waters fill the sea, the earth will be filled with an awareness of the glory of the Lord" (Habakkuk 2:14). You can't look at the sea without seeing water everywhere. God wants the knowledge of his glory seen everywhere.

So this glory that we see in God and receive in us makes us

missionaries. I'm calling you to embrace this aspect of God's glory. You are not your own; spend your life to bring glory to God.

The Vehicle of Glory

I see planting house churches as the vehicle God uses to glorify Christ.[1] What does planting house churches have to do with glorifying God?

In some places, planting churches is nothing more than an exercise in developing a group to lead. Many church plants in the West simply create worship services that attract Christians from other churches. Often, a church starts with solid motives but morphs into just one more option for people who are dissatisfied with their current house of worship. Many great things can happen in these churches; a few people will even come to Christ. But in the end, the number of Christians in a city remains unchanged because believers are just moving from one place to another.

Instead, I'm calling you to plant a church birthed out of God's glory. Plant a church that is born when unbelievers—friends, family, acquaintances, or co-workers—see God's glory in you and in Christ. As this happens, that glory moves inside them and reproduces in them. They, in turn, live a different life that draws the attention of others around them, and the cycle of glorifying God in another believer continues. The purpose of planting house churches is to spread the knowledge of the glory of God to as many people as possible.

House churches planted among lost people are easily reproduced, so they quickly spread. One house church can turn into two or three in a year's time. Individuals from one house church can be launched to quickly plant another house church. While we say that numbers are not important, we gain a new perspective when our focus is right: Every new lost person who submits to Christ is another person who is now glorifying God.

Every new house church is a new community made up of

new believers experiencing God's glory for the first time. God's glory is increasing with each step. Forming churches among the lost is not easy, but glorifying God is worth it.

Chapter 3: The Calling of Christ

For we are His workmanship, created in Christ Jesus for good works, which God prepared beforehand, that we should walk in them.
~ Ephesians 2:10 ESV

[He] gave himself for us to redeem us from all lawlessness and to purify for himself a people for his own possession who are zealous for good works.
~ Titus 2:14 ESV

By this point, you're probably ready to tell me that you aren't called to start a church. "I'm not a pastor," or "I haven't been trained to start a church," are a couple of excuses that people give. We have been taught to think about calling and training in ways that exempt us from following Christ into the mission field.

But reconsider your calling in light of the harvest. God intends to show his glory to every person on the planet. He has chosen his church as one of the primary vehicles of displaying his glory on Earth. Every single Christian is part of that church and part of the plan to reveal God's glory. Are you a follower of Jesus? Then you are called.

The Great Commission (Matthew 28:18–20; Acts 1:8) was originally given to the apostles, but it was not just for the apostles. They were to teach everyone to obey what Jesus commanded, including the commandment to make disciples. Those disciples were to make more disciples, both nearby (in Jerusalem) and far away (to the ends of the Earth). The gospel was always moving from person to person and place to place. Ordinary people were swept up into the army of believers who saw their role in taking the gospel to places it had never been. They were not a static church; church was not just a place you went on Sunday. Instead, the church was a movement designed to continue spreading the gospel and recruit other recruiters. And you are called to be part of this movement.

Regardless of your specific calling, we all have a general calling: to reproduce followers of Jesus. In 1 John 2:12–14, John wrote about three different life stages in the Christian walk: children, young men, and fathers. Your walk with Christ includes a progression that mirrors biological maturing. First, you're a child, learning to know the Father. Then, you are a young man (or woman) who is fighting battles against Satan. But few people ever reach the third stage.

In the third stage, you are a spiritual parent. In this stage, one births, raises up, and gives life to another generation. We are typically told that we need more training before we become a spiritual parent and that this stage is only for a select few. But I believe this stage is the inheritance of every child of God. Every believer has a place in this movement, but some of us have been told there is no room for us or that we're not called.

Think about that. We expect our children to grow into young men and women. We expect young men and women to become functioning adults. If a thirty-year-old man never grows beyond the maturity of a six-year-old, something is wrong. The vast majority of young people become parents. In the same way, we should expect many, if not all, believers to grow up to become functioning spiritual mothers or fathers to spiritual sons and daughters.

I'm telling you, we need you. I'm telling you, the church needs more people to step into the place of fathers and mothers. I'm telling you, you are called to this. I'm declaring to you what Jesus has been saying for two thousand years. The harvest needs you.

Jesus's Invitation

At one time in the life of Jesus, the power of God from him drew multitudes. (See Matthew 9:35–38). Matthew tells us that Jesus looked out at the crowds and had intense compassion for them because they were confused and helpless like sheep without a shepherd. Just like the people of Nineveh, these people did not know their right hand from their left, and Jesus's heart was broken for them. (See Jonah 4:11.)

What was his response? He called his disciples and showed them the masses. His words, spoken almost two thousand years ago, remain timelessly true: "The harvest is great, but the workers are few. So pray to the Lord who is in charge of the harvest; ask him to send more workers into his fields" (Luke 10:2). Jesus's response to the enormous harvest was to ask the disciples to pray for more harvest workers to come forth.

And this is where we begin. We start in our calling by seeing the enormity of the harvest. When I entered one of my more fruitful ministry seasons, the Lord took me up to the highest floor of my college and had me look out the window and pray. Over and over again, I would see what he saw in this passage: the people going about their lives, lost and astray. And it provoked me to pray.

Take some time to think about how many people are on the planet right now. Possibly 2 to 2.5 billion people claim the name of Jesus.[1] We also know that not all of those are saved. So that leaves at least 5 billion people on a path to destruction. The harvest is so huge that you and I are a tiny drop in the bucket compared to the vast sea of lost humanity.

But friend, Jesus calls us to pray in response to this situation. Let your heart travail in prayer over the condition of fallen humanity apart from Jesus. And learn to pray the prayer Jesus taught us to pray: Lord of the harvest, raise up laborers for the harvest field.

The Prayer That Is Also an Invitation

But that's not the end of the story. No doubt, the disciples prayed the prayer that Jesus instructed them to pray. But what they did not and probably could not understand was that the invitation to pray was also an invitation to be sent.

You see, the very next thing that happens in Matthew 10:1 is that Jesus calls his twelve disciples and gives them the authority to take part in the harvest. This is key: The very ones Jesus told to pray for workers to be raised up become the very workers as an answer to the prayers they prayed.

This happened to me. During that season at my college campus, he moved me to pray. But as he moved me to pray, I began to get his heart for bringing the gospel to my campus. This became one of my most fruitful times of ministry. Many came to the Lord as I became the worker in answer to the prayer God was leading me to pray.

What does this mean for you? If you can see the harvest, if you can see the need and connect with how absolutely lost humanity is, if you can be moved with compassion along with Jesus and join him in prayer for more workers to be raised up, then you are probably the worker you've been praying for.

After being exposed to the compassion of Jesus's heart and after praying with him to raise up laborers in the harvest field, you are being invited to be a laborer yourself. You may have a specific function or role to play, but take your place as a laborer alongside Jesus in the harvest.

Welcome to the Movement

You might be wondering, "But can't I take part in the harvest as part of an established church?"

The simple answer is yes. The more difficult, more truthful answer is that the churches we have are not bringing the gospel to the lost quickly enough. In many churches, the gospel is stagnant and not spreading from person to person as God designed.

Jesus's answer to this was not to keep all the apostles together and create the first church of Jerusalem. It was to send out missionary groups to proclaim the gospel of the kingdom. These groups would find houses of peace and declare the gospel of the kingdom to all those there. These houses of peace that accepted the gospel would become house churches.

Even though the church stayed in Jerusalem for the first eight chapters of Acts, persecution eventually scattered it. And in that stage of scattering to the different cities and towns of Judea, Luke says, "The believers who were scattered preached the Good News about Jesus wherever they went" (Acts 8:4). From there, we rarely see those first disciples all in the same place. God's Word was supposed to be spread, which meant that people needed to move around. They had to leave their place of comfort and go to a new, unfamiliar place.

These weren't just the seasoned apostles either. In Acts 8, Phillip, one of the servants we see in Acts 6, is preaching and establishing churches. In Acts 11, a no-name group of "believers who had been scattered during the persecution after Stephen's death" started the church in Antioch (Acts 11:19). This church launched Paul and the expansion of Christianity to Europe. And it was started by an unnamed group.

Movements of the gospel must move. And for them to move, people, whether or not they are certified apostles, must move from where they are to somewhere else. As obvious as this seems, joining Jesus in this movement will mean you move.

The lost aren't coming to your church. Even if they are, that is not our commission. Our commission is to go and find the lost (Luke 15:3–7). "Go into all the world and make disciples" is much different than staying within the walls of your church and making disciples of the lost who come to you.

This does not mean you dislike your church. It means you are obeying the commission of Jesus to make disciples where there aren't any. It means, like Jesus, who left the face-to-face fellowship of the Father, who left literal heaven to reach dying humanity, you're leaving the immediate fellowship of your existing church to reach captives of the enemy where they are.

The calling is to take the gospel where it's not. Don't stay, go. Make disciples where people respond. Because the harvest is great. Because the laborers are few. Because the Lord of the harvest is sending out laborers into his harvest field. Because Jesus is worthy of the reward of his suffering.

Calling Comes First

"But I'm not equipped. I'm not ready."

You're right. You're probably not equipped or ready. But Jesus has this disturbing habit of picking people who aren't ready. He doesn't call the equipped; he equips the called.

Stop for a second and think about the guys who were the first fruits of this laborers' prayer. None of them were equipped. Sure, they left their lives to follow Jesus. But none of them were ideal church planters. They were fishermen, tax collectors, and revolutionaries. None of Jesus's disciples were trained as Pharisees. None of them had spent their lives studying the Scriptures. But he still called them.

In fact, the only religiously trained follower of Jesus who started churches was a very violent man named Saul. He would later write, "Remember, dear brothers and sisters, that few of you were wise in the world's eyes or powerful or wealthy when God called you" (1 Corinthians 1:26).

Think about this: Who in the Bible was ready for the call of God when it came? Most of the truly called people were surprised. Some even rejected the call at first. Most were not qualified by the standards of those around them. That is what made them the perfect choice. No one was expecting Saul the Christian killer to become Paul the church planter. No one was expecting Gideon, hiding in a pit, to be the deliverer of the nation. No one was expecting fishermen like Peter and James and John to turn the world upside down.

So you might not be the ideal ministry candidate. That's what makes you so perfect for working among the lost. That enables you to build bridges with those who know nothing about Christ. You are not the ideal candidate, which makes you ideal. "The Lord doesn't see things the way you see them. People judge by outward appearance, but the Lord looks at the heart" (1 Samuel 16:7).

You Are Called

The harvest is great. The laborers are few. Jesus is asking you to pray for more laborers. As you do, you become the answer to that prayer.

You are called! Don't say no to the calling because you aren't equipped. Say yes to a God who is infinitely wiser than you are. Say yes because the power of God is stronger than all your imperfections and reasons for saying no.

I've been telling you over the past few chapters that this is a dangerous calling. This calling will bring all your fears, insecurities, and reasons to give up to the surface. Jesus must be more valuable than your fleshly need for safety and security.

You will need to be sure you are called. It's the only way you will stick your neck out.

Chapter 4: An Easily Planted Church

And you are living stones that God is building into his spiritual temple. What's more, you are his holy priests.
~ 1 Peter 2:5

All the believers devoted themselves to the apostles' teaching, and to fellowship, and to sharing in meals (including the Lord's Supper), and to prayer.
~ Acts 2:42

Let's be clear: I'm asking you to plant a church. But don't let the picture of the church you come from scare you away from this call. You may not be able to start that kind of church, and even if you can, the friends you lead to Jesus won't be able to start that kind of church. I'm asking you to start a church like you've never seen before.

The church I'm asking you to start is simple. It doesn't need a paid pastor, a building, or even a worship leader. It is so simple that high schoolers and the homeless could start one. The ideas are so simple that they can be written on the back of a napkin and followed. We're intentionally trying to keep this simple.

While house churches are simple, they are not easy. Paul was able to walk into cities, preach the gospel, and gather a church in a matter of weeks. The unlearned, the "not many wise," became leaders in these churches. With house churches, the process is not complicated. You don't have to have extensive training; you just have to be willing to lay down your life.

Back to Basics

A lot of smart Christians will tell you that the first church met in an upper room in Acts 2. But I believe that the first church started in Mark 3. Why? Here, Jesus not only chose twelve disciples to heal the sick and cast out demons, but he chose twelve men to be with him. If the church is a group of people who follow Christ, learn from him, and learn to do what he did, this is the first expression of church that we see in the New Testament. Don't miss this: The church began as a group of ordinary people in a relationship with Jesus.

This church was so simple; it met as it went. Much of Jesus's teaching during his life comes from this first church that existed in the relationships between these thirteen men. They learned how to pray, how the Old Testament applied to their lives, and how to cast out demons, heal the sick, and lay down their lives. They did all this without a building or without any religious education.

This was Jesus's leadership style. He was practical. He was more concerned about the hearts of men and the gospel reaching all the Earth than he was about establishing a religious center. Interestingly, Jesus's last command was not to buy buildings and train people to have religious ceremonies. His last command was to take the gospel to the ends of the Earth and make disciples. He trained the twelve in the gospel of the kingdom. After his resurrection, he trained them to do the same thing and disciple others.

So when the Holy Spirit fell in Acts 2 and God finally came to live in the human heart, the church didn't build a building, hire pastors, or start seminaries. They were a church on the move. They met wherever they were. Yes, that meant early on, they met in the temple, but they also met from house to house. This church did not exist in one place. It existed in the relationships that the people had with each other. It was a reproduction of the first church that Jesus started when he called the twelve disciples to himself. This church made disciples wherever they went. It was obedient to the Great Commission.

These churches quickly grew and multiplied. The persecution *and* growth rapidly dispersed the church, and they no longer met in the temple court. Now, they mostly met house to house. Churches became groups of families, friends, and neighbors who had submitted to Jesus. These churches met in homes that were the center of these relationships for encouragement and strengthening. This is why Paul frequently wrote epistles to the church of a city, such as Colossae or Rome, and at the end of the book, he greeted, "Aquila and Priscilla (for example) and the church that meets in their house."

We need to return to this example. These churches spread so quickly because they were based on the essentials—Jesus and relationships with his followers. They did not require a lot of money or expertise. They met regularly in the house of a key person—what the Bible calls a "person of peace." It was the simplest way to provide a gathering space.

Today, we call this form of meeting a "house church." This type of church is important because it allows the focus of the church to be on Jesus and making disciples. We don't have to plan sermons, finance buildings, or figure out how to pay pastors. The construction worker, the high schooler, or the retiree can plant this type of church. Since anyone who follows Jesus can plant a church, they spread.

While this church is based on relationships, these relationships must regularly come together to encourage and strengthen each other. If they don't, the people who make up this church will quickly become weak or distracted and fall away. The church in Jerusalem met daily together for this very reason. Make no mistake, the church needs to hold a consistent and intentional gathering to encourage believers.

The Essential Practices

What do these churches do when they gather? Luke records four main practices of the early church, and Paul adds yet one more. Luke tells us in connection with these practices that the church grew daily. We need to rediscover these practices as part of the pathway to a church that grows daily.

We learn these practices from the early church and form the basis of what happens when the church gathers. These churches do a few simple things when they meet. They devote themselves to the apostles' teaching, they fellowship with each other, they eat together, they pray, and they serve each other with their gifts. (See Acts 2:42 and 1 Corinthians 14.)

Devoted to the Apostles' Teaching

The apostles had personally learned from Jesus. In the book of Acts, they were the only direct link the church had to the teachings of Jesus. But the apostles' teaching was more than just the words they said. Specifically, the apostles' teaching was the gospel that Peter had just proclaimed in Acts 2. They gathered to rehearse the gospel to each other and encouraged each other in its truths.

While we practice teaching in the church, rarely do we focus on the good news of the kingdom and the death and resurrection of Jesus. While this involves teaching, we need to be clear that this is not just a three-point sermon. Recently I heard a story about a church planting movement of illiterate Africans who had spread the gospel far and wide with only about thirty memorized Bible stories. They didn't know much, but they devoted themselves to what they knew.

My point is not that we can't go deep in Scripture but that we don't need an extensive knowledge of the Bible to produce strong disciples. The gospel of Jesus produces strong disciples. When we gather as a church, our job is to talk about the gospel, to remind each other how it applies to our lives, and to call each other to be faithful to it. This is the heart of devoting ourselves to the apostles' teaching.

In our church, we practice this by bringing our Bibles when we meet. Often someone shares what the Lord has been speaking to him or her. If no one brings a specific teaching, then we crack open our Bibles and read through a certain book together. Often the Holy Spirit highlights how that section applies to us as individuals or to the whole church. It requires no prepared sermon; God will speak to you as you all read the Bible together.

Devoted to Fellowship

The first-century church didn't just gather for massive teaching and preaching sessions. Remember, these churches met in homes, not just for a worship time but to eat and spend quality time together. This was more than just a casual gathering spent playing games or consuming entertainment. They shared their lives, worked together, cried together, and encouraged each other. Paul wrote to the Thessalonians, "We loved you so much that we shared with you not only God's Good News but our own lives, too" (1 Thessalonians 2:8).

For this reason alone, not everything about a house church can be structured. We have to allow for interruptions, for kids to make noise, for hearts to be hurting and need attention. Think of the last time your family got together. You possibly met for a purpose, but you enjoyed a lot of spontaneity as you loved and interacted with each other. So don't program your house church. Make space for human and Holy Spirit interaction. Make room for everyone to talk, share, and encourage each other. The quiet will have to learn to speak up, and the talkative will have to learn to listen.

I can't tell you the number of times that a seemingly random comment or action in our house church meeting opened up space for someone to share their heart for the whole church to see. Instead of shaming the person, this became an opportunity to minister to them. Likewise, birthday parties or group work projects became moments for discipleship, accountability, and encouragement. If we spend time together, we will grow as a body.

One final note: If you truly want a deeper connection with others, your church will naturally meet more than once a week. Intentional and spontaneous meetings will occur throughout the week as friendships blossom and grow. Jesus will show up, not just in the intentional meetings but when you informally gather together. This is healthy and should be encouraged.

As an example, tonight is Friday. On Friday nights, my wife and I go out on a date and let a couple from our house church watch our kids, or the other couple goes on a date while we watch their kids. Tomorrow, I will meet with leaders from our house churches in the morning to pray. In the afternoon, I will go out with another brother to share the gospel. On Sunday, our house church has a scheduled meeting, but we may do something fun together that day as well. I'm back to work on Monday, but I'll have lunch with someone from our house church that day. On Wednesday, someone will come over, and we'll talk about their budget after dinner. Thursday night, someone from our house church will host kids from our neighborhood at their house. The point is, it's hard to tell where life ends and church begins.

It should be like that.

Devoted to Eating

The early church was dedicated to eating together. This wasn't just a random occurrence. They intentionally made time to gather and eat food as spiritual families.

The reason they did this was because Jesus modeled it, and they learned it from him. He was known, not just as someone who hung out with sinners, but as the guy who was constantly eating and drinking (Luke 7:34). For Jesus, eating and drinking was a way to bridge gaps between people who would otherwise never come together. When you ate with someone in that time, you were saying that you wanted a relationship with that person.

Anyone who has ever eaten at a middle school cafeteria knows that not much has changed in two thousand years. We still show our acceptance toward one another by eating with them. The early church made a practice of eating together that became an expression of an accepting, peace-making society. Rich, poor, slave, and free all sat and ate together, expressing that Jesus could take the most different and divided people and unite them.

Communion was also practiced at this meal. In the same way that Jesus gave the first communion at the end of the Passover meal, the early church shared communion after a true meal together. A loaf of bread and wine were passed around the table as the culmination of a dinner.

Go back and look at how the Corinthians celebrated the Lord's Supper. They had enough food and wine there to either save people from going hungry or for people to get drunk (1 Corinthians 11:21). In this passage, Paul is no doubt referring to communion, because he rehearses how the Lord gave the apostles the first communion right before he was betrayed (1 Corinthians 11:23–25) as an example for the Corinthians to follow. The Corinthian example ties back perfectly to the Last Supper where Jesus sat, surrounded by His friends, enjoying a full meal (Matthew 26:20–21). During the meal, Jesus passed bread and wine to those around the table and led them in the first communion (Matthew 26:26–29). They even shared together in worship (Matthew 26:30). Paul acknowledges that the Corinthian meal was modeled after Jesus's Last Supper but called them to enjoy it in a holy way that bettered the community.

Our house churches practice this by eating together and sharing the gospel as we take communion around a common table with a meal. We break the bread and pour out the juice as the culmination of the meal and talk about how Jesus gave his life for us.

Eating together, including the Lord's Supper, can be a powerful reminder of the gospel every time we meet.

Devoted to Prayer

The early church didn't only turn to prayer when life became hard. They devoted themselves to prayer. They walked out the practice of prayer in their daily lives together. Everyone was constantly praying.

Jesus had taught the apostles that they could ask for anything in his name and he would give it to them. He even told them this would be the basis for doing greater works than he did. So when the church gathered, they put this promise into practice. They prayed for what they needed, believing that the resurrected Jesus would answer their prayers.

It's tempting to minimize the place of prayer as just a quaint activity, but prayer and relationship with Jesus fuel the church. Churches that grow weak in prayer inwardly begin to shrink and die. As Francis Chan says, "If prayer isn't vital for your church, your church isn't vital."[1] Churches that pray bring God into their situations and see miraculous results that could never come by their own efforts.

When our church gathers, we pray. Often, we will ask if anyone needs prayer and pray for the needs people mention. We often have several needs that only God can fix. So we bring those to God together when we gather.

House churches should also spend time praying for the church and for the harvest. The only way we will get to the place of growing spontaneously like churches did in the book of Acts is if the church gives itself to this type of prayer. We must devote time to asking God to send out more laborers, bring in the harvest, and to strengthen the church. The prayers Jesus, the apostles, and Paul prayed in the Gospels, Acts, and the Epistles are a model for how the early church prayed.

Paul's Addition

The previous four practices were Luke's description of the early church when it met. Paul shares one other description of what happens when the church meets in 1 Corinthians 14. When the church meets together, everyone brings a supernaturally inspired gift to contribute to the gathering: a song, a teaching, a message in tongues, an interpretation of that message, etc. The point of all this is that everyone else who hears or sees what is happening is encouraged to grow in their faith.

Sharing our gifts is the other simple element of house churches. The church gathers to encourage each other, which happens when the body learns to serve each other with their gifts. Because the body is constantly in flux, parts of the body will be strong, and another part will be weak. Those who are strong have the job of encouraging those who aren't.

While I think Paul would encourage us to share all our gifts, the kinds of gifts Paul specifically has in mind here are those that are supernaturally inspired by the Holy Spirit. Prophecy, defined as hearing God speak to us, can demonstrate God's reality to an unbeliever in the meeting. A message in tongues, including supernatural translation of an unknown language, can strengthen the church. Gifts of healing show God doing what only he can do.

Imagine a meeting of the church when it was clear that God was speaking. Believers who were discouraged could once again believe that God knew their situations and was acting on their behalf. Believers who were sick were made whole by the power of Jesus. One person shares an unintelligible message that another person can miraculously interpret. Wouldn't you walk away from a meeting like that encouraged? Wouldn't your faith be strengthened? Wouldn't you be encouraged that the gospel is powerful and able to change people? So Paul encourages us all to bring our gifts to the meeting.

This happens by being open to the Holy Spirit. Every believer should be spending time with the Lord privately and, prior to meeting with others, ask Jesus how he or she can serve the body. If the Lord shares anything with you, when you gather, discuss or act on it. During the meeting, you can keep asking the same question.

As an example, we have often had new believers join our fellowships, and each time, we pray over them. It's not unusual for this to turn into a time of prophecy and for our new guests to shed tears of joy as the Lord speaks through one or more of the people present. Physical and emotional healings of all types have also happened.

Jesus wants to show up and reveal himself in our meetings as we gather. By sharing what Jesus is showing us, together, we point to him in a greater way than we can on our own.

Simple Church

What does it take to plant a church like this? We simply need to gather believers in a central location (typically a house) at an agreed-upon time. Those who started the house church can instruct and model believers on a few of the important functions of house churches: discussing the apostles' teaching, fellowship, eating, prayer, and serving others with our gifts. Then, we simply do these week in and week out.

As the weeks progress, some of these disciplines will be emphasized more than others as the needs of the church change. But as we devote ourselves to these practices, those who are present will grow up in the grace of Jesus. As they do, the gospel will go forth, and other churches will be planted.

Not only can you start a church like this, but your newly saved friend can probably do it too. This is the beauty of the house church model: Very few can be a popular preacher or even lead a church of two hundred. But almost everyone can meet with other believers and do these simple practices. This type of church is easily planted and replicated.

We could plant churches that are more complex, but that would mean fewer people could start them, and it would also mean fewer laborers. The church Jesus started could be planted by simple, uneducated men who loved Jesus with all their hearts. Our goal should be to plant this easily started type of church so that as many laborers as possible can end up on the harvest field and the gospel can reach more people.

Can you help others understand the gospel? Can you share your life with others? Can you eat with others? Can you pray? Can you share your spiritual gifts? If the answer is yes, then you can start a house church that helps bring glory to Jesus and helps spread the gospel to the darkest parts of the planet.

The question is, "Will you?"

Chapter 5: Character That Carries a Movement

For many are called, but few are chosen.
~ Matthew 22:14 ESV

Do your best to present yourself to God as one approved, a worker who has no need to be ashamed, rightly handling the word of truth.
~ 2 Timothy 2:15 ESV

I was not disobedient to the heavenly vision.
~ Acts 26:19 ESV

Jesus began a movement that was designed to spread from Jerusalem to every nook and cranny of the planet. The simple gospel was intended to be passed from person to person and people group to people group, leaving churches in its wake. Each of these churches should be a planting ground for a new group of missionaries to learn how to bring the gospel to others.

I'm inviting you to take part in a house church planting movement that reaches the lost wherever you are. For this house church movement to truly spread, we need people with the character to sustain it. Skill and enthusiasm can start churches, but without character, these churches will quickly sputter and die.

Character Sustains Kingdom Movements

How does character sustain a movement? Since the people of God—not a building, organization, or event—are the church, the only things that bind them together are Christ and their relationships to one another. Relationships require love, trust, and transparency to thrive over time. Others will quickly lose trust in church planters who lack the character of Jesus. Love then grows cold and transparency disappears. When people lose trust in each other, the church will die.

Jesus was convinced of this. He regularly invited everyone to take part in kingdom activities but had high standards for those who decided to join. He told a story of a wedding feast when a great king invited all his subjects, but many rejected the invitation. The king sent messengers out to the furthest parts of the kingdom and invited anyone who would come to the party. Many came, but when the king arrived, he had some thrown out because they weren't prepared for the wedding party. Jesus ends the story with this statement: "Many are called, but few are chosen." (See Matthew 22:1–14.)

The kingdom is like this. Many are called. Many are invited into the kingdom, but few prepare themselves for the standards they find inside. Those who embrace the standards of the kingdom end up producing real, long-term fruit.

Neil Cole and Church Multiplication Associates have a saying that speaks to this well: "We want to lower the bar of how church is done and raise the bar of what it means to be a disciple."[1] A church can be simple and reproducible if we make sure that we are reproducing quality disciples full of the character of Jesus. One won't work without the other.

Not only does Jesus say it, but I have watched it happen. Over the years, I have seen house churches rise and fall based on the character of those involved. I have watched men and women with mixed motives shipwreck the lives of others because of defects in their character.

I have also seen men and women who long to be used by

God ask him to search their hearts and purify their lives. Regardless of how much pain and sin was in their background, these people have grown to be like Jesus and helped others find Christ and grow in him.

The difference was not how sinful each person's past was. Most of these men and women came from rough backgrounds. The difference was who was willing to pursue Christ-like character and submit themselves to Christ and his body in the shaping of their hearts. Those who were willing found that God changed and used them.

Paul says it like this to Timothy: "Do your best to present yourself to God as one approved, a worker who has no need to be ashamed, rightly handling the word of truth" (2 Timothy 2:15 ESV). "In a wealthy home some utensils are made of gold and silver, and some are made of wood and clay. The expensive utensils are used for special occasions, and the cheap ones are for everyday use. If you keep yourself pure, you will be a special utensil for honorable use. Your life will be clean, and you will be ready for the Master to use you for every good work" (2 Timothy 2:20–21). Our ability to be used by the Master is related to the quality of our character.

What matters right now is not that you are perfect, but that you are pursuing God. Do not let the fact that you aren't perfect stop you. You might be dealing with some issues that need to change. You might have areas of your life where you feel guilt and shame, but right now, you can begin to trust in the love of Jesus and walk away from past sin, guilt, and shame. Right now, you can start to pursue the kind of character that will make you effective in God's kingdom.

A Different Kind of Character

What kind of character are we talking about? I'm not asking you to become a nicer person, more like Mr. Rogers. Instead, I'm asking you to pursue the character that, at its root, displays a radical submission to Jesus. If our simple gospel is "Jesus is

Lord," then the simplest definition of the character that I'm calling you to expresses Jesus's lordship in every area of your life.

What does that look like for a church planter? What is the top bar of discipleship that Jesus calls us to? Let's take a look at the following essential areas: being disciples, being faithful, and being submitted.

We Must Be Disciples

Jesus sent committed disciples to be a part of his kingdom work. A disciple is learning to follow the example of another. In biblical times, a disciple would leave their parents and study under a teacher to learn their way of life. Christian disciples are those who are learning to follow Jesus as their *Way* of life.

Jesus said it like this: "If any of you wants to be my follower, you must give up your own way, take up your cross daily, and follow me" (Luke 9:23). Disciples of Jesus have given up doing things their own way. They have decided to learn from Jesus, both as he is revealed in Scripture and as he reveals himself to them personally. These disciples have also learned the value of the community of Jesus to help them discern Jesus's way from their own.

We must also be willing to take up our cross. For some of us, that will mean physical loss of life. For others, it might mean losing a job or being mocked for following Jesus. Some of us will be inconvenienced for the sake of others who have come to Christ. Regardless, we are disciples when we are ready to bear the pain of the ministry Jesus called us to. Jackie Pullinger, a great missionary to the drug addicts of China, says it like this: "The gospel is always death for the one who brings it, and life for the one who receives it."[2] Disciples embrace the pain of the mission they join Jesus in.

Lastly, disciples follow Jesus. The early apostles had to do more than merely leave their fishing business or their tax collecting; they had to follow the man, Christ Jesus. It's not enough to only sacrifice, but we must enter a daily relationship with Christ where we do what he tells us to do. When Peter and John were released from prison, threatened, and told to never speak of Jesus again, all the apostles found strength in prayer to continue the spread of the gospel. Peter was in prayer when the Lord showed him a vision of unclean animals he was supposed to eat. When Peter finally understood what this vision meant, the gospel was released to the Gentiles. Paul and Barnabas were ministering to the Lord in fasting and prayer when Jesus sent them as apostles to the Gentiles. We must set aside time to hear his voice and do what he's asked us to do.

I cannot emphasize this enough: Our ability to give up our own way, take up our cross, and follow Jesus is not merely the most mature version of discipleship—it's discipleship 101. We must first embrace the life of being a disciple before we try to make disciples of others, or we will run the risk of making disciples of ourselves instead of disciples of Jesus. Without the lifestyle of discipleship, the rest of our pursuit of character will be a lifeless obligation. When we become disciples, the pursuit of character becomes a joy. This is what makes discipleship the most essential character trait.

We Must Be Faithful

Those who give themselves to the lifestyle of discipleship become disciplined people. They learn to follow Jesus consistently over weeks, months, and years, and this consistency is called faithfulness. Being faithful means that God and others can count on you to act a particular way over a long period of time.

Faithfulness expresses to others the likeness of God. For so many, the world is chaotic and unpredictable. Even our own families have been unpredictable—sometimes good and selfless and sometimes evil and selfish. As the church, we are called to be a model family after the good, kind, and consistent character of God. God is a good Father who never changes, so we get to model being good brothers and sisters to each other, people who can be counted on.

Faithful people are easy to spot because you can count on them in the area they are faithful in. A faithful worker will show up to work on time every day and consistently work. A faithful evangelist will always preach the gospel to lost people. A faithful farmer will continue to tend the crops every day, believing that the outcome of his labors will be a harvest.

Church planters are faithful, show up consistently, pray regularly, share the gospel repeatedly, and make disciples of those who respond. They are the sort of people you can count on in a crisis and are available when you need to talk. Faithful church planters use their time wisely and are available when possible to other disciples and lost friends and neighbors.

Last night, on Christmas, we had just pulled into our driveway from celebrating with the family when my wife's phone rang. She didn't recognize the number but answered the phone anyway. On the other end of the line was the boyfriend of a lost friend of hers. He was worried about our friend and spent about twenty minutes on the phone expressing his concern. What made the boyfriend of our friend feel free to call on Christmas night? It was the faithfulness of my wife over the last several years to love this couple sacrificially. Faithfulness builds bridges of trust that others eventually feel the freedom to walk across.

So how do we become faithful? Faithfulness means to be full of faith. A faithful person believes that God is good and he will reward our obedience and seemingly insignificant efforts with an eternal reward, regardless of the earthly outcome. (See Hebrews 11:6.) Some of the great heroes of the faith died without seeing the fullness of the promise they believed God for. (See Hebrews 11:13.)

The faith that we are successful—apart from results—frees us to influence the Earth. Just like the farmer who tends his crops, expecting a harvest, we continue to sow the good news and the good works of Jesus into the lives of others. Not every seed will sprout into conversion, but we know if we sow liberally, more seeds will sprout than if we don't. This liberal sowing makes us more effective because we can trust Jesus with the outcome of our sharing.

Churches will thrive when the people who start them and take part in them continue to show up with God's good news and good deeds. Each time we share the message of Jesus or demonstrate the kingdom, we teach people that God is faithful to meet our needs. God builds a kingdom people through this process.

At times, you and I will be unavailable. These become critical opportunities for our churches to learn to trust in God and not in the church planters. The church now has the opportunity to be faithful in the same way we modeled faithfulness.

We Must Be Submitted

House churches are built on relationships and not on top-down organizational structures. This helps everyone take part and contribute to the life of the body, but it can also encourage spiritual excess or a failure to confront sin. The way to safeguard churches from this is to encourage a culture of submitting to one another.

In traditional churches, a pastor or maybe a team of elders often leads. Everyone is used to submitting to that person or team of people because they are the ones in charge. They're responsible for helping us stay out of trouble, and we are supposed to submit to them. The New Testament calls us to something higher though: to live lives submitted to the other brothers and sisters in our spiritual families. This is why Paul told everyone in the church at Ephesus to submit "to one another out of reverence for Christ" (Ephesians 5:21 ESV).

Paul's encouragement to the Ephesians was to revere or honor the presence of Christ in every single person within the Ephesian house churches. No one was above another, no one below another, just fellow believers who each had Christ within them. The Ephesians were supposed to submit under Christ. Instead of one guy monitoring everyone's life, the whole church took responsibility for one another.

I was once in a gathering of believers where the most senior leader had taken a group of guys and had a short devotional. A group of us were there; some, serious in our faith; some, not so much. One older man was known as the joker. He was never serious, either about life or about faith. Yet I watched as the Holy Spirit moved on him powerfully in that meeting, and he began to encourage and exhort the most senior leader in that movement. The beautiful thing was that the senior leader was able and willing to receive correction because he honored Christ by receiving from this other brother. Like this leader, we all need to be willing to revere the life of Christ in other believers, not just those we think are the most spiritual among us.

This submission to other brothers and sisters strengthens our churches from sin and heresy. We are often lousy at self-examination, and we all have blind spots. Our willingness to listen and respond to the instruction, encouragement, and even correction of other brothers and sisters helps us avoid the weaknesses in ourselves we can't see.

I will warn you now that all sorts of unruly people are drawn to new, relational churches. They will look to co-opt what God is doing in your midst and draw people after themselves or some new teaching. What will identify them is their refusal to submit to the body. You safeguard your house churches by walking this out well in front of them in the earliest days.

For this very reason, I recommend you plant churches with another believer who is not your spouse. Of course, your spouse should come along too, but you need another brother or sister so that you can model submission in front of new believers. They will learn mutual submission from you and the other brother or sister, and they will be much more willing to practice listening and learning from you and each other if they see you and another believer practice it in front of them.

How do you begin to grow in this character trait? Get an accountability partner of the same gender who will eventually plant a church with you. Meet with them weekly. Share your sins and pray for each other. Be real with each other instead of just glossing over surface issues. Help each other follow Christ better. Learn to submit to this other believer for your good. Do this well, and you will model it for others. It will make all the difference in the churches you start.

This partner will help you examine the critical parts of your life. None of us are perfect. If we were, we would not need the gospel. Instead, we need help to identify our areas of weakness and continue to work on them before we begin starting house churches. You need enough credibility in each area to make you a stabilizing force as the gospel goes out. Are you thinking about divorcing your wife? You need to reprioritize and focus on your marriage before you try to plant churches. Are you struggling (as all parents are) with some aspect of your kid's behavior? You need to grow in this area and make sure you are submitting to Christ. But this should not stop you from starting a new church. There is a delicate line to walk here, which is where it becomes helpful to be part of a transparent community where it is okay to be vulnerable with your weaknesses. This kind of church is God's assessment tool to help you figure out how ready you are.

Pillars in God's House

God is positioning you to provide stability to the house of God. Those who start churches should have the type of character that matches the church's calling to be "a pillar and foundation of the truth." The church must stand against corruption and for what is good and true about Jesus. This will require you to have an excellent reputation.

When Paul wrote to his church planting partner Timothy, he described the kind of character that every person needs as a stabilizing force among people coming to Christ. The person needs to have the following attributes: "They must be above reproach, the husband of one wife, exercise self-control, live wisely, and have a good reputation. The person should love people who are different from them and be hospitable, must be able to teach, must not be a heavy drinker, or be violent. The person should be gentle, not argumentative, not greedy, and must manage their household well, having children who respect and obey them. They must not be a new believer and have a good reputation outside of the church" (1 Timothy 3:2–6, my paraphrase).

People who live lives like this while starting new churches among the lost help provide examples to new believers of what maturity looks like. They bring wisdom and maturity to what is often a young, undisciplined atmosphere. Movements without these pillars can descend into chaos.

I'm sure as you read this list, you feel disqualified in an area or two or even ten. But instead of becoming discouraged, take this opportunity to grow. Bring the area where you feel unqualified to Jesus and talk to him about it. Confess your weakness to your accountability partner and ask for his or her help in growing in that area.

Many Are Called, Few Are Chosen

Jesus invites everyone to take part, but not everyone prepares themselves to participate like they need to. The point of this chapter is not to talk you out of church planting—quite the opposite! The harvest is plentiful, and the workers are few. Come take part but also ready yourself to participate.

Look at your life. Are you a disciple of Jesus? Have you left your old life behind? Have you denied yourself? Are you encountering and responding to Christ daily? Are you faithful in what God has called you to? Are you submitted to other believers in the body of Christ? Are you growing in the areas of character Paul wrote to Timothy about?

If the answer is yes, then join us. If the answer is no, get with a trusted friend and begin working through the issues of the heart where you are stuck. If the answer is, "I don't feel qualified," resolve these matters with a friend. However, make sure you're not seeking unreasonable perfection before you step out.

Qualification does not mean perfection. An honest friend with some maturity will be the best person to tell you whether you are stalling or if your life needs some serious work.[3]

Remember, the harvest is great. The workers are in short supply. We have a staffing issue that we keep asking God to fix, and you may be part of that solution. Don't let your insecurities stop you. If work needs to be done, let the power of God's love and the urgency of the work push you to get to the root of your character issues. Don't wait for someday because it often never comes.

Don't settle for not being part of the harvest that God is releasing in this hour. Regardless of what you think holds you back, Jesus is ready to remove barriers in his pursuit of the lost people on this planet. The question is, will you join him?

Chapter 6: Calling Forth the Women

Give my greetings to Priscilla and Aquila, my co-workers in the ministry of Christ Jesus.
~ Romans 16:3

Now I appeal to Euodia and Syntyche. Please, because you belong to the Lord, settle your disagreement. And I ask you, my true partner, to help these two women, for they worked hard with me in telling others the Good News. They worked along with Clement and the rest of my co-workers, whose names are written in the Book of Life.
~ Philippians 4:2–3

We've written so far about the need of the hour—the harvest is plenty, and the workers are few. We now need more workers for the harvest. Because of this, we haven't gotten specific about who can or can't start house churches, except to say that we want people with the evidence of following Jesus in their lives. If the harvest is plentiful but the laborers are few, then we need every available hand to bring in the harvest Jesus promised us.

Yet we often exclude a large group of people from the discussion about planting house churches. Knowingly or unknowingly, women are often not thought of as viable agents whom God can use to expand his kingdom. This must change. We need every part of the church sharing the gospel, making disciples, and building communities in the kingdom—including women.

Women, I need to be clear about this. You may have theological concerns, you may not think you are capable, or you may simply not know how you can fit church planting into your schedule, but I can assure you of one thing—we need your help.

Why We Need You

I remember the day clearly. We had just multiplied our first house church and released that new family to minister on the outer edge of our city. Those remaining with us had hearts for the inner-city neighborhood where we lived. I looked around the room at the mix of men and women and young children, and we talked about what it might look like to more effectively sow the gospel in our neighborhood.

In the middle of the discussion, I felt the prompting of Jesus, and I began to tell the women that we needed them. Our neighborhood was full of single moms who knew the struggle of raising large families all on their own. "Women, we need you. The men will be a part of reaching this neighborhood, but we will need you women to spread the gospel. It will spread because of you and the relationships you make with other women here. You'll end up mothering girls that have no moms and showing other moms a better way."

This came true in many ways. One woman became the perfect party planner, helping us become a people of kingdom celebration and abundance in a world of lack. All the women became surrogate moms and aunties for the young women we would encounter. We spread the gospel through conversations, coffee, and birthday parties. We would not have shared the gospel with nearly as many people if it weren't for the women in our house church.

Now think about that scenario that I just described. Single-parent households. Kids who had never known their fathers. Kids who looked up to women. What five or ten years ago characterized the inner cities is now characterizing our entire culture. The need for women to be on the front lines of sharing the gospel, discipling those who have come to Christ and forming spiritual families, has only increased. And that trend doesn't show signs of slowing down anytime soon.

Jesus Radically Includes Women

For those women who have grown up in the church, one of the big questions isn't whether they want to but whether they believe Jesus and the church wants them to be involved in this process. Many have grown up in a church culture that only allowed men to do most things, especially related to leadership, while the women were left to care for the kids and teach women's Bible studies.

This is a huge discrepancy from what the New Testament teaches. You will be hard-pressed to find stories in the New Testament of women just tending the house and the kids. Yes, they *did* that, but they also did much, much more.

Let's start with Jesus. While we know that Jesus had twelve male disciples who followed him around, we also know that women played a significant part in his ministry. He had no regular job and no home to speak of. His travel seemed to be funded at least in part by a group of women who he'd significantly impacted: "Soon afterward Jesus began a tour of the nearby towns and villages, preaching and announcing the Good News about the Kingdom of God. He took his twelve disciples with him, along with some women who had been cured of evil spirits and diseases. Among them were Mary Magdalene, from whom he cast out seven demons; Joanna, the wife of Chuza, Herod's business manager; Susanna; and many others who were contributing from their own resources to support Jesus and his disciples" (Luke 8:1–3). The women who had encountered Jesus and were changed by him were traveling with him and helping finance his ministry.

Jesus also seemed to have a strong relationship with Mary and Martha of Bethany along with their brother Lazarus. Martha was known for taking care of the house and hosting Jesus and his disciples. In one story, Martha attempts to rebuke Mary for not helping her tend the house. Jesus's response to Martha is that Mary had chosen the good part, something that would never be taken from her. What was Mary doing? Was she sitting starry-eyed, looking at Jesus and thinking of a restful, spiritual state in heaven? Was she just being "so heavenly minded that she was no earthly good?" No! Luke tells us that Mary "sat at the Lord's feet, listening to what he taught" (Luke 10:39). She was positioning herself in the place of a full-fledged, participating disciple. She saw her place in God's kingdom and prioritized that over the typical domestic concerns and even restrictions that parts of Christianity assign to women.

Need more examples? Jesus's birth starts with a holy, humble virgin who says yes to an angel who came with a mysterious message (Luke 1:38). His ministry begins as that same woman, now older, insists her miracle son do something about the party that ran out of wine (John 2:1–12). He spent an unprecedented amount of time speaking of the kingdom to one woman at a well by herself, partly because he loved and cared for her and partly because she was key to reaching a whole Samaritan village (John 4:1–42). Mary Magdalene was the first person Jesus sent to others to announce the news of his resurrection.

Yes, Jesus mostly taught with and worked with his male disciples. So while these stories of women don't demand our focus, the fact is that they do exist. This should cause us to stop and re-evaluate if we've sold Jesus short on what he would allow a woman to do in the name of expanding the kingdom.

The Early Church Radically Included Women

Jesus's disciples continued his inclusion of women in church ministry. Women were part of the prayer meeting that preceded the arrival of the Holy Spirit in the upper room (Acts 1:14). They believed that their "daughters [would] prophesy" (Acts 2:17), and they did (Acts 21:9). A woman named Tabitha had a ministry serving the poor and others (Acts 9:36). Her illness, death, and resurrection became the basis for the spread of the gospel throughout her region. Now, this would happen with anyone who died and was resurrected, but she was well-known in the city for her service to others. Other women who came to Christ opened doors for significant ministry in an area. God opened the heart of a woman like Lydia (Acts 16:11–40) or God-fearing women in Thessalonica (Acts 17:4).

Let's not forget, either, that the apostles also traveled in teams with their wives, which Paul says that Peter, the other apostles, and the Lord's brothers did (1 Corinthians 9:5). Now, in the West, when we think of women traveling with their husbands in ministry, we think of hotel rooms, airline flights, and luxury. This was not the New Testament understanding of apostolic travel. It was a hardship with the potential to be robbed, left out in the cold, or even die. These women who traveled with their husbands were not treated to a luxury trip; they were responsible for participating in the hardships of ministry with their husbands.

Paul wrote of a similar reality. His letters to the churches were filled with acknowledgments of his female co-laborers. Phoebe was a servant of the church in Cenchrea (Romans 16:1). Paul uses the word "deacon" to describe her role, which is elsewhere in the New Testament used to describe Paul himself, Timothy, Apollos, and other members of his apostolic team. In that same letter, he acknowledges Priscilla, the wife of Aquila, as a co-laborer (Romans 16:3). He recognized Mary as a hard worker for them, which actually meant that she was a co-laborer in the gospel. Junia was a woman who was highly respected among the apostles and *possibly* even considered an apostle herself (Romans 16:7). He also acknowledged Tryphena and Tryphosa, whom he calls the Lord's workers, and Persis, whom he says had worked hard for the Lord (Romans 16:12).

This wasn't just a unique situation in Rome. In many places where Paul greets the church by name, he names women who were helping him spread the gospel. The letter to Philemon is also addressed to Apphia, a woman and possibly Philemon's wife, in Philemon 1:2. In Philippians 4, he appealed to Euodia and Syntyche to reconcile with each other, but, in the process, acknowledged that each of them "worked hard with [him] in telling others the Good News" (Philippians 4:2–3). In his letter to the Colossians, Paul greets Nympha and the church that met at her house (Colossians 4:15).

One of the clearest examples of a woman working to host and mother a church in the New Testament comes from the book of 2 John. This book is written to the chosen lady and her children. Commentators are split as to whether they believe this was a literal woman or an image for a church that had many disciples (children) because the whole letter involved church matters. I believe both are true. John wrote to a real woman who was likely a natural and spiritual mother. The church that probably met in her home was an extension of her family, so while the letter was sent to a literal person (a woman) and her children (probably both natural and spiritual), these matters were to be handled as a church, because they were a church. The entire book of 2 John was written to a church most likely started and hosted by a woman.

The Elephant in the Room

With all this said, it is time to address the elephant in the room. In several places throughout the New Testament, Paul writes that women are not to teach or have authority over the men (1 Timothy 2:11–14) nor are they supposed to speak in a church gathering (1 Corinthians 14:34–35). These passages form the major argument against women in ministry and women in any church leadership capacity. The debate has raged in churches for decades now, and because of that, women have been sidelined.

I will not pretend to offer a new perspective that will end this debate. I want to leave the interpretation of these passages to you and the church where you belong, but you need to understand that these passages aren't just isolated teachings. Paul gave these instructions to the churches in the context of co-laboring women who shared the gospel, endured hardship, built up the church, and hosted churches in their homes.

Look at this great example from one of the more problematic passages. In 1 Corinthians 14:34, Paul tells the Corinthians that women should remain silent during a church meeting, and if they have questions, ask their husbands at home. If we only read 1 Corinthians 14, we might believe this meant a woman shouldn't say anything when a church meets together. When we read 1 Corinthians as an entire book, though, we find that Paul specifically instructs the conduct of women when they pray and prophesy (1 Corinthians 11:5).

While Paul's teaching in 1 Corinthians 14 seems to show a simple truth about women not speaking in church, the larger context of 1 Corinthians causes us to view those verses in a slightly different light. We need to look at all of Paul's teachings on women and their activity in the church in the context of everything he said about the women who were fully engaged in winning souls, discipling converts, and sending workers.

Paul allowed women to serve the church through evangelism, discipleship, and church planting. Paul's theology was not misaligned with his strategy. He was not hypocritically teaching the Corinthians or Timothy something he wasn't practicing. Regardless of what those passages mean, Paul clearly wanted women to be part of God's plan of expanding and establishing his kingdom.

Calling Forth the Women

So what about you? You, the single young lady. You, the wife and young mother. You, the older woman in the faith who has raised her children. What about you? Do you have a place in the expansion of God's kingdom? I believe you do.

Don't let the fact that you are a woman keep you from what God is doing. First-hand testimonies coming back from the underground church of China tell us that somewhere between half and two-thirds of the church planters there are women. Most of them are between the ages of eighteen and twenty-four.[1] This is not happening in the safe, supposedly progressive West but in a country where imprisonment is the reward for preaching the gospel.

If our Chinese sisters are spearheading the spread of the gospel in such an environment, surely women in the West are much more capable than we give them credit for. So yes, you have a place, dear sister, in the spread of the gospel. You can share Jesus with those around you. You can disciple those who want to follow him. You can host a church in your home or apartment where believers can work together to build each other up and reach more people. It's your inheritance, too—not just the men's!

What is important is not your gender or the level of experience you have in ministry. What is important is that you are seeking to obey Jesus and follow him. What is important is that you have a heart full of love for the people around you and you want to see them come to Jesus. These are the genuine qualities of the heart that make house churches thrive.

My dream, sisters, is that you would find your place in what God is doing in bringing in the great harvest. I do not want you to wait around for a brother in Christ to get brave and take the lead. My dream is that you would hear the call for laborers and respond to Jesus. Become a laborer in his harvest. You can do this! The gospel is too important, the hour is too late, and the need is too great for you to wait for a man to give you permission to do this important work. Instead, begin, just like the men reading this book. Say yes and see what God will do.

Mordecai told Esther, "Who knows if perhaps you were made... for just such a time as this?" She was a young Jewish girl called to save the nation of Israel when no man could. (See Esther 4:14.) This was not just a statement to provoke her to action; it was to encourage her when what she was about to do might cost her, her life. What lies in front of you is an invitation to join with the men in the kingdom of God on the inconvenient, hard, and sometimes dangerous work of spreading the gospel by multiplying house churches. With the harvest as ripe as it is and the laborers so few, perhaps you too were born for such a time as this.

Chapter 7: Wanted: Workers for the Harvest

The harvest is great, but the workers are few. So pray to the Lord who is in charge of the harvest; ask him to send more workers into his fields.
~ Jesus, Matthew 9:37–38

You and I were born for the harvest. Jesus's words are as real today as they have ever been. A great harvest of souls is still happening across the planet. Atheist and Muslim countries that seemed closed to the gospel a decade ago are seeing significant numbers of people turning to Christ. All over Africa and Asia, and now even in Europe, and Central and South America, the fire of the gospel is spreading. The cultural West, long celebrated for sending missionaries all over the world, will once again become a hotbed of missional activity and see a great harvest. You get to be a part of this spread of the gospel.

To do so will require much from you and the others who join you. It begins with a fresh surrender to Jesus as the king of your life. He will be the defining reality in it, not your dream, nor the dream your nation or your parents had for your life. This fresh surrender will cost you everything.

What you get back in return, though, will be the ability to pursue the glory of Jesus in a way that will multiply and spread across the planet. He will give you the immense privilege of partnering with him to see his glory spread. You will start in your neighborhood, but the gospel you share will be shared and shared again until it reaches places you have never imagined.

God will bring glory to himself as the gospel is spread like a virus. This will happen as simple, reproducible churches multiply again and again. People from your house church will start another one. That one will start two more. And on it goes until we reach the ends of the Earth with the good news of Christ dying to save humanity.

This will happen because you—yes, you—are called to make disciples. That means sharing the gospel with the lost, equipping new disciples, and even parenting the churches that form as these new disciples gather. You will mature from just another believer into a mother or father in the faith who has raised up spiritual families of disciples.

It will happen because the type of church you will plant won't have four walls and a complicated structure. You are planting a viral gospel through a church that can be "sneezed" into existence. You can share the gospel, give some guidance on how to meet as a church, and coach that church, and it will prosper and grow. It will have a life of its own. This church will meet wherever its people are. It doesn't need seminary-trained leaders. It just needs you and people who are willing to follow Jesus.

It will happen because you have done the hard work of character formation with Jesus. This means you have decided to follow in the footsteps of Jesus. You have decided to become consistently faithful and live a submitted life, both to Jesus and to close friends, Christ-followers who can attest to your character. The gospel will continue to spread because you have a changed character that attests to its power.

Perhaps it will also spread because our sisters in Christ will awaken to their part in God's plan to bring in the harvest. Half of the body of Christ will finally be permitted to function. Before, spiritual mothers felt as if they didn't have a role in the church, but now, they can raise a whole new generation of disciples through the churches they start.

The need of the hour, my dear brothers and sisters, is

workers. For too long, the body of Christ failed to fully engage those who have called on the name of Christ. Can you imagine an industry where, once an employee was hired on for life, that employee never went on to do any work for that business? How would that business do? What about a business where the model employee showed up on time and as scheduled but sat back and watched others do the job? That business would not last long.

No, God is looking for laborers—those who are willing to lay down their lives, their reputations, their convenience, their sense of entitlement, their comfort, and even their safety so that the gospel will go forth. They will work regular jobs, enjoy life with their spouses, and take care of their kids, but beyond all that, they desire to see Jesus glorified in the eyes of people who don't know him.

Laborers, Come Forth

I am calling forth a rare form of worker in Christianity today, a worker willing to embrace the dangerous work of taking the gospel to hard places. The churches needed in these environments will be small, nimble, flexible, and organic. They most likely cannot pay the person who starts them, so I'm calling forth volunteer workers who will support themselves as they make disciples. The only reward for planting these churches will be the reward that comes from Jesus.

I am calling forth workers who will be faithful in the face of disappointment and heartbreak. Not everything will go your way. Yes, people will come to Jesus. But people will also walk away from him in this process. Those who showed the most promise one day may betray you the next. I am calling forth those who love Jesus to serve the lost and the church because they love him above everything else. This is what makes them steady and causes the church to flourish.

I am calling forth workers who will pioneer churches that will not be understood in many places. These churches will be about relationships, not programs. They will meet everywhere and anytime. They will break from some of the inherited traditions that many churches have accepted as ordained by the Lord. For this reason, some Christians will look down on those. Others will try to recruit them. The workers I am calling forth will have to soldier on without the approval of others, understanding that they serve to please God and not men.

All of this, dear brothers and sisters, is part of the costly task of planting house churches in the Earth today. These organic house churches are God's vehicle for spreading and increasing the glory of Jesus across the globe, but the external and immediate rewards are few. The harvest is great, meaning we need many more house churches that will raise up more and more disciples. This will require more laborers.

I cannot guarantee safety. I cannot guarantee revival. I cannot ultimately guarantee success. I can only guarantee that if you say yes to Jesus and to the Great Commission, you will come alive in a way you haven't before, and you will receive a heavenly reward that far outweighs anything you leave behind.

Are you willing to join me in the dangerous life of planting house churches? Will you surrender to Jesus with me as we give our lives to the spread of the gospel and the making of disciples? Will you leave behind comfort, glory, honor, and safety to see the gospel touch people who would never darken the door of a church building? Will you work to see disciples who make disciples who make disciples?

Then I invite you, brothers and sisters, to join me in the task of spreading and reproducing the gospel. I invite you to join me in starting house churches among people who previously did not know Christ. I invite you into the life of multiplying house churches all over the planet.

I invite you, dear reader, to stick your neck out.

Appendix A: When Not to Start a House Church

I wrote *Stick Your Neck Out* to provoke others to leave the comfort of their current experience and follow God in planting a house church. However, as I've watched house churches grow, mature, and even die, I've come to realize that some people shouldn't start a house church, at least not yet. If you find yourself in any of the following situations, wait until the situation is resolved before you try to start a house church.

- God tells you no or to wait.
- Your spouse or nuclear family is not in agreement with your decision.
- You are currently struggling with a mental health issue that makes you a danger to yourself or others.
- Your decision to start a house church will cause pain or division with an existing, Bible-believing body of believers, whether they are a house church or a traditional church.
- You have a recent history of broken relationships without reconciliation. I define "recent" as within the last eighteen months.
- You are running from your previous church. Leave your previous church body in peace as much as possible, preferably with the blessing of your leaders.

- You have a difficult time with submission to others.[1]

If you find yourself in any of these situations, please wait to start a house church. The nature of the work requires someone called by God, with a supportive spouse and family, with solid mental health, who wants to build and not harm the body, and who will not bring a lifestyle of toxic relationships into new disciples' lives.

Knowing when you are out of these situations is harder than you think. I would recommend finding a faithful and objective friend of the same gender to talk to about your situation. Be brutally honest with that person about what you are dealing with and why you think it will hinder your ability to start a house church. Give them permission to ask questions and hold you accountable. Invite them to tell you when they think you are ready to launch out and start a house church.

The harvest needs you, but it doesn't need a damaged person damaging others in the process.

Appendix B: Further Reading

My goal in writing this book has been to encourage you to launch out in the mission God has called you to by starting a house church. I've intentionally kept this book light on the how-tos of house church instruction because plenty of books are out there on the topic. The great need of the body of Christ (in the West, at least) is not another book about what a house church is and how to lead one but an invitation to take action with all the information we already have.

With that said, it's not lost on me that after reading this invitation, you may need more information. If you would like to read further on the subject of house churches, I would invite you to read the following books that have been helpful to me on my journey:

Chan, Francis. *Letters to the Church*. Colorado Springs: David C. Cook, 2018.

Cole, Neil. *Organic Church: Growing Faith Where Life Happens*. San Francisco: Jossey-Bass, 2005.

Rohde, Ross. *Viral Jesus: Recovering the Contagious Power of the Gospel*. Lake Mary, FL: Passio, 2012.

Simson, Wolfgang. *Houses That Change the World: The Return of the House Churches*. Milton Keynes, Bucks., UK: Authentic Media, 2004.

Yun, Brother. *The Heavenly Man*. Oxford, UK: Monarch Books, 2002.

Zdero, Rad. *The Global House Church Movement*. Pasadena, CA: William Carey Library, 2004.

Notes

Chapter One: Stick Your Neck Out
1. Throughout this book, I use the terms "start a church" and "plant a church" interchangeably.
2. Billy Graham, "Billy Graham Speaks: The Evangelical World Prospect," *Christianity Today*, October 3, 1958, https://www.christianitytoday.com/ct/1958/october-13/billy-graham-speaks-evangelical-world-prospect.html.
3. Fenggang Yang, "Christianity's Growth in China and Its Contributions to Freedoms," Georgetown University, October 31, 2017, https://berkleycenter.georgetown.edu/responses/christianity-s-growth-in-china-and-its-contributions-to-freedoms.
4. VergeNetwork, "Alan Hirsch – Every Believer a Church Planter," YouTube Video, 0:40, August 20, 2010, https://www.youtube.com/watch?v=oE-8rgg0G-0.

Chapter Two: The Glory of Christ and the Planting of Many House Chuches
1. House churches are not the *only* way to glorify God. We glorify God through praise (Psalm 147:12; Luke 2:20);

by doing good works so that others glorify God (Matthew 5:16); and through the preaching of the gospel (Acts 13:48). Even so, church planting represents a significant impact that is largely ignored in the conversation of how to glorify God.

Chapter Three: The Calling of Christ

1. "Christians," Global Religious Futures, access date January 5, 2020, http://www.globalreligiousfutures.org/religions/christians.

Chapter Four: An Easily Planted Church

1. Francis Chan, *Letters to the Church* (Colorado Springs: David C. Cook, 2018), 79.

Chapter Five: Character That Carries a Movement

1. Neil Cole, *Organic Church: Growing Faith Where Life Happens* (San Francisco: Jossey-Bass, 2005), 26.
2. Jackie Pullinger, "Death to Self," Sermon Index, 37:29, accessed January 5, 2021, https://www.sermonindex.net/modules/mydownloads/singlefile.php?lid=11537&commentView=itemC.
3. For more clarity on whether your situation would exclude you from starting a house church, see Appendix A: When Not to Start a House Church.

Chapter Six: Calling Forth the Women

1. Jo Anne Lyon, "Both Men and Women - An article on "Spirit-filled Believers" from Jo Anne Lyon," Weslyan, September 30, 2013, https://secure.wesleyan.org/227/both-men-and-women-an-article-on-spirit-filled-believers-from-jo-

anne-lyon. See also J. Lee Grady, "Where Are the Women of Fire?" CBE International, accessed January 11, 2021, https://www.cbeinternational.org/resource/article/mutuality-blog-magazine/unheralded-and-unknown.

Appendix A: When Not to Start A House Church

1. This list is not exhaustive. Many other situations could present themselves that should serve as warning lights before an individual proceeds with starting a house church. For more on this topic, refer to Chapter 5.

About the Author

Travis Kolder is a church planter with 15 years of experience in starting, growing, and sustaining house churches. He has started at least five local house churches and coached several church planters long-distance. He lives in eastern Iowa with his wife, Christy, their six kids, and one grandchild. He graduated from the Forerunner School of Ministry in Kansas City and now works full-time as a loan officer. In addition, Travis serves the Cedar Rapids House Church Network. He also stays up too late at night reading, writing, and thinking about church planting movements.

Connect with Travis in the following ways:

Traviskolder.com

@traviskolder (Twitter)

Facebook.com/traviskolder

Made in the USA
Monee, IL
06 March 2022

92359816R00046